JUN 15 '07

16.95

D0119113

DATE DUE

WITHDRAWN

BLAZERS

The U.S. Armed Forces

The U.S.
Air Force
Thunderbirds

by Carrie A. Braulick

Consultant:
Barbara J. Fox
Reading Specialist
North Carolina State University

Capstone
press

Mankato, Minnesota

Blazers is published by Capstone Press,
151 Good Counsel Drive, P.O. Box 669, Mankato, Minnesota 56002.
www.capstonepress.com

Library of Congress Cataloging-in-Publication Data
Braulick, Carrie A., 1975–
     The U.S. Air Force Thunderbirds / by Carrie A. Braulick.
     p. cm.—(Blazers. The U.S. Armed Forces)
     Summary: "Describes the U.S. Air Force Thunderbirds, including their planes,
the maneuvers at their air shows, and team member duties"—Provided by publisher.
     Includes bibliographical references and index.
     ISBN 0-7368-4392-2 (hardcover)
     1. United States. Air Force. Thunderbirds—Juvenile literature. 2. Stunt
flying—Juvenile literature. I. Title: United States Air Force Thunderbirds. II. Title.
III. Series.
UG633.B725 2006
797.5'4'0973—dc22   2004027806

Credits
Juliette Peters, set designer; Patrick D. Dentinger, book designer; Jo Miller, photo
     researcher; Scott Thoms, photo editor

Photo Credits
Art Directors/Maxwell Mackenzie, 25
Corbis/George Hall, 17; William Manning, 22–23
DVIC/SRA Greg L. Davis USAF, 12, 19
George Hall/Check Six, 14 (bottom), 26
Getty Images Inc./AFP/Kim Jae-Hwan, 6, 7
Photo by Ted Carlson/Fotodynamics, 13, 14 (top), 28–29
Photri-Microstock, cover, 11
USAF Air Demonstration Squadron, Media Relations, cover (inset); SSgt. Sean
     White, 5, 8, 19 (inset), 20–21, 27
Zuma/Art Seitz, 18

**Capstone Press thanks MSgt. George F. Jozens, public affairs superintendent,
U.S.A.F. Thunderbirds, for his assistance in preparing this book.**

1 2 3 4 5 6 10 09 08 07 06 05

Table of Contents

The Thunderbirds in Action

The Thunderbird planes glide into the air. People in a large crowd are excited for the show to begin.

★ ★ ★ ★ ★ ★ ★ ★ ★ ★ ★ ★ ★

Four planes fly beside each other in the diamond formation. They make a large loop.

Opposing knife-edge pass

The pilots continue showing off their exciting moves. Later, the show ends. People in the crowd rush to meet the pilots.

BLAZER FACT

In American Indian legends, Thunderbirds were large creatures that made the earth shake when they flew.

Thunderbird Planes

The U.S. Air Force Thunderbirds perform daring moves with planes. Their first planes were Thunderjets.

Thunderjets

★ ★ ★ ★ ★ ★ ★ ★ ★ ★ ★

Today, Thunderbirds fly F-16 Fighting Falcons. These fighter jets are fast and easy for pilots to control.

BLAZER FACT

Many pilots call F-16s "Vipers."
As F-16s land, some people
think they look like pit
viper snakes.

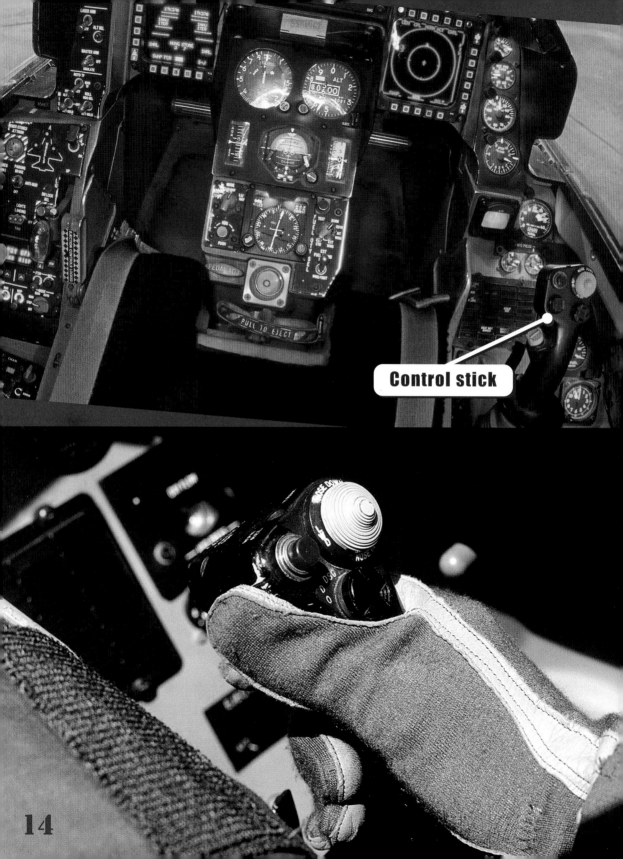

Control stick

Pilots use cockpit
equipment to fly the planes.
They use a control stick
to change directions.

Maneuvers

High-speed maneuvers are the heart of a Thunderbird show. Rolls, loops, and dives thrill crowds.

Bomb burst

Many maneuvers include formations. The delta formation is shaped like a triangle. Four planes make an arrowhead formation in the arrowhead loop.

Delta

BLAZER FACT

The Thunderbirds' delta formation is named after the fourth letter of the Greek alphabet.

Arrowhead

19

Crossover break

Sometimes, one or two planes are the center of attention. In the crossover break, two planes cross paths.

Delta Positions

Commander

Left wing

Right wing

Lead solo

Opposing solo

Slot

Thunderbird Jobs

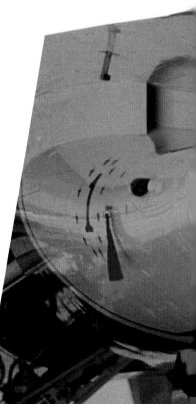

The pilots in shows are not the only Thunderbirds. Other team members fix planes, plan shows, and do other jobs.

All Thunderbirds train for their jobs.
New pilots learn each maneuver before
they fly in shows. Skilled pilots keep
shows both exciting and safe.

Bon-ton roulle

27

Flying in the diamond formation

Glossary

cockpit (KOK-pit)—the area in the front of a plane where the pilot sits

control stick (kuhn-TROHL STIK)—the lever in a plane's cockpit that a pilot uses to steer

delta (DEL-tuh)—the six-plane formation of the Thunderbirds

diamond (DYE-muhnd)—a formation in which four Thunderbird planes form a diamond shape

fighter jet (FYTE-ur JET)—a fast plane designed to destroy enemy aircraft

formation (for-MAY-shuhn)—a group of planes flying together in a pattern

maneuver (muh-NOO-ver)—a planned and controlled movement

roll (ROHL)—to turn sideways in a complete circle

Read More

Donovan, Sandra. *The U.S. Air Force.* U.S. Armed Forces. Minneapolis: Lerner, 2005.

Gaffney, Timothy R. *Air Show Pilots and Airplanes.* Aircraft. Berkeley Heights, N.J.: Enslow, 2001.

Hopkins, Ellen. *The Thunderbirds: The U.S. Air Force Aerial Demonstration Squadron.* Serving Your Country. Mankato, Minn.: Capstone Press, 2001.

Internet Sites

FactHound offers a safe, fun way to find Internet sites related to this book. All of the sites on FactHound have been researched by our staff.

Here's how:

1. Visit *www.facthound.com*
2. Type in this special code **0736843922** for age-appropriate sites. Or enter a search word related to this book for a more general search.
3. Click on the **Fetch It** button.

FactHound will fetch the best sites for you!

Index